HOT FAT

Russell Alford & Patrick Hanlon

CONTENTS

INTRODUCTION

There's a certain alchemy when something delicious is submerged in hot oil. It fundamentally changes – texture, colour, size, even aroma – creating a wonderfully crisp edible barrier, cooking from the outside in and locking in juiciness.

Hot fat truly captivates us and the process of deep-frying has become a fervent fascination. The shattering crunch of battered fish; pillowy soft doughnuts yielding to teeth, covering lips in a saccharine sprinkle; the benchmark dual texture of proper chips with a lightly crisp, golden exterior and fluffy interior, drawn lavishly through thick mayonnaise or gravy. We all love to order and eat deep-fried delights in restaurants, fast food joints, markets and food trucks, but why have we become so averse to and anxious about heating fat to cook at home?

Chefs will tell you that texture is everything in a complete dish. A dish doesn't need to be complex to be complete, but a combination of textures brings layers of enjoyment, intrigue in each forkful. Beyond taste and flavour, texture adds a whole other sensory element to food enjoyment. Think about the dimension an icy granita brings to a chilled dessert or how a lusciously spoonable sauce slicked over and around roast chicken brings composite parts harmoniously together. Consider why we seem to always serve crackers or oatcakes and slices of sharp green apple with cheese. It's *all* about combining textures rather than providing your mouth with the same thing to endlessly chew, taste and swallow.

Our goal with this book is to enable you to peer beyond the curtain (or cornet) of chips and captivate you with a long, rich, delicious pathway of fried joy that lies ahead.

Buttermilk fried chicken burger

BC (BEFORE CHIPS): THE HISTORY OF DEEP-FRYING

While batches of colourful glazed doughnuts and stacks of onion rings are de rigueur on Instagram, the history of deep-frying goes further back in history than you might think and has evolved through the centuries. Rudimentary deep-frying of dough (like fritters and beignets) can be traced back to parts of the Middle East and Classical Greece before arriving in Europe in the Late Middle Ages. It wasn't until the fairly recent late 18th century that potato batons (an early form of the modern 'French fry') began to be sold on the Pont Neuf in Paris.

Fast forward to the mid-20th century and the fast food revolution roared, with golden arches cropping up across continents and a globally connected world where traditions, flavours and cuisines can be shared, implemented, adapted and enjoyed effortlessly. Fast food – for all its flaws in quality, provenance and overindulgence – has made deep-fried food almost an everyday thing, accessible whatever the budget.

EVERYTHING IN MODERATION...

Look, Oscar Wilde said it best: 'Everything in moderation, including moderation.' Don't go overboard, but don't unnecessarily limit yourself either – and by that we mean limit your own joy. Food is joy, food is nourishment, food is culture, food is history, food is creativity and food is fulfilling. Even cooking itself is all about balance, an equilibrium of sweet, salt, sour, bitter, texture and temperature. We know which philosophy we'll be firmly following.

Spoiler alert: in the coming pages we're not going to disclose a calorie-free way to deep-fry food, but we're also not expecting a reader to make this their everyday, weeknight culinary bible. We'd like this to be a little bit of what you fancy. We'd like to share a book that is joyful, full of deliciousness, a treat for the tastebuds and the senses and an opportunity to truly indulge every so often in crave-worthy crunch.

DEEP-FRYING SAFELY

To deep-fry, you ideally need a deep-fryer. Yes, it's a clunky bit of kit, but it's quite inexpensive, with varying sizes and shapes to suit all requirements and budgets. It isn't essential, but for ease – and most importantly, safety – it is recommended.

Pot-frying can work but you must have a reliable thermometer. Regulating the temperature to keep it consistent is a skill that takes a bit of practice, but it's totally achievable. If you're not using a dedicated deep-fryer, a large, wide pot or casserole (Dutch oven) can be used with a thermometer, but avoid filling it more than two-thirds full, as the combination of the food, its coatings, the temperature and how full the pot is can cause a sharp increase in volume and the oil could spill over.

1 **Oil and water do not mix, ever.** Ensure whatever you're frying is patted dry (if it's not coated or battered) or the splashes can cause the oil to 'spit' and result in small burns.

2 **Never leave hot oil unattended**, especially if you aren't using a deep-fryer. The temperature can increase rapidly, close to and beyond smoking point, and hit the flash point where it becomes fire. As long as you're monitoring the temperature, using the correct amount of oil and being attentive to what's happening, you shouldn't have issues.

3 **If the oil begins to smoke**, turn off the heat and let it cool down. If a fire does begin, especially with a pot of oil, turn off the heat and smother the flames with a tight-fitting lid or a baking tray that fits over it. If you have an appropriate fire extinguisher, use that. Whatever you do, never spray the oil with water or the flames will spread. If anything like this happens while using a deep-fryer, inform the manufacturer, as the temperature shouldn't go beyond the maximum of 190°C.

4 **We recommend deep-frying in a well-ventilated kitchen**, either with the windows open or the extractor fan on.

Oil, lard, dripping – when you heat any form of fat, it all becomes liquid gold in our book. But not all fats are created equal. Where flavour is concerned, animal fats are superior, especially pork lard and beef dripping, but they can be difficult to source in bulk or in sufficient quantity for your basket or saucepan capacity – not to mention a nightmare to clean as they solidify quickly once cooled, which is very bad for the fryer's heating element. They also carry a heftier price tag than standard plant-based oils.

All the recipes in this book have been tested with either sunflower oil, vegetable oil or both. Except for some rare occasions, the two are interchangeable. A wonderful thing about deep-frying at home is that you're in control of your ingredients, which includes your choice of oil.

Vegetable fats (oils)

Rapeseed oil Also known as canola oil, cold-pressed is best. It's widely available and used for a variety of cooking techniques, like olive oil but with a more neutral aftertaste.

Peanut (groundnut) oil This oil has a noticeable nutty flavour and scent and is low in saturated fat. Choose unrefined and cold-pressed where possible.

Sunflower oil A neutral, clear oil pressed from sunflower seeds, mostly produced in Eastern Europe.

Grapeseed oil A by-product of winemaking, oil extracted from *Vitis vinifera* grapes will always be refined rather than unrefined in order to be palatable. As a high source of fatty acids, a very high smoke point and slightly cheaper than EVOO, it's a good all-rounder.

Olive oil A refined version of the oil extracted from olives (most commonly in the Mediterranean countries of Spain, Italy, Portugal and Greece) that's suitable for frying, though it's recommended to use it only once.

Animal fats (oils)

Beef dripping is rendered beef fat that is solid and hard at room temperature with a pronounced, deep beef flavour. **Pork lard** and **tallow** (usually from aged mutton) are similar forms of animal fats. While these are great for deep-frying in theory, they aren't great for the deep-fryer itself – or the person who has to clean it, at least! Perfect in a heavy-based pot with a thermometer though.

DISPOSING OF OIL

To dispose of your spent oil, pour the cooled oil into the original tub or bottle it came in via a jug and funnel, if required. Many recycling centres take cooking oil, so check with your local authority to see if they offer that service (it's often used as a form of biofuel). But whatever you do, never pour oil down the drain, either inside or outside the home. This causes serious plumbing issues, notably large 'fatberg' blockages, and the last thing we want is a sewer blockage to get known as the Hot Fatberg.

A NOTE ON AIR FRYERS

One of our biggest pet peeves with the entire air fryer concept is the fact that the word 'fry' is in the name of this kitchen implement at all. In essence, an air fryer is a countertop oven blowing warm air over food, so it's more closely related to your standard oven than your deep-fryer. A similarly clunky, useful piece of kit, of course, just don't get them confused and definitely don't expect the same results. Would you make a cup of tea in a toaster? No.

We attempted to test as many of the recipes in this book as possible in an air fryer and let's just say we're doing you a favour by not recommending that many of them be replicated in one. However, what we will say is that it's a seriously quick and useful piece of kit for reheating fried food (chips, fried chicken, prawn toast, etc.) without it going soggy.

INGREDIENTS AND RECIPE TESTING

All eggs used in these recipes are large and free-range or organic.

Throughout, we recommend using the best-quality ingredients you can afford, but we especially encourage you to use free-range or organic chicken. Free-range pork can be more difficult to source, but is worth seeking out. All beef used is Irish grass-fed beef.

All recipes have been tested at least three times in a home kitchen, adjusting quantities, temperatures and processes to ensure you achieve the best results and can rely on each one of these recipes in your frying repertoire.

HOMEMADE CRISPS

Sure, you can pick up any number of packets of crisps in wild varieties of flavours in every shop and supermarket, but there's something incredibly satisfactory about making your own crisps at home. We take this omnipresent convenience staple for granted, but make your own and you'll not only have a new skill, but a newfound appreciation for your go-to savoury snack. To our American friends, we will never call these 'chips', and you, in turn, will likely never sway from using the term 'fries' for what we know as 'chips'. It's just one of those language anomalies, but let's all stay frying friends.

3–4 medium-sized potatoes

1 tsp fine sea salt, plus extra for seasoning

sunflower oil, for deep-frying

Peel your potatoes, then slice them very thinly with a mandolin. Get a large bowl of cold water and stir in the teaspoon of salt, then add the potatoes and leave them in there for about 20 minutes.

Heat the oil in your deep-fryer to 170°C.

Shake the excess water off the potato slices and pat dry. Working in batches, gently place the slices individually into the hot oil. Try to avoid slices sticking together, as they will likely want to.

Fry for 3–4 minutes, shaking the basket constantly or using a spider or slotted spoon to turn them around in the oil. They will become quiet and float towards the surface as they reach their optimum point, but they continue to cook – and can easily overcook, over-colour and soak up a lot of excess oil – so don't be too complacent.

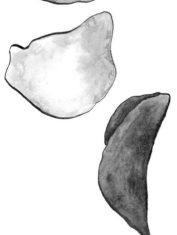

Shake the basket to rid them of excess oil, then tip out onto a flat surface lined with kitchen paper. Place the crisps into a large mixing bowl and season with salt, shaking excessively to ensure an even coating. Transfer the crisps to another bowl to avoid those at the bottom becoming soggy. Leave until ready to eat.

TOP CRISP TIPS

USE A MANDOLIN

You need a mandolin to slice the potatoes thinly enough to make this work, otherwise you'll just end up with circular chips.

TRY HERITAGE VARIETIES

If you're lucky enough to get your hands on some colourful heritage potato varieties, such as those grown by Maria and David Flynn of Ballymakenny Farm in Ireland's bountiful Boyne Valley, use them! Stunning dark indigo-hued Violetta and electric pink-coloured Red Emmalie make the most visually appealing crisps. However, other options to seek out are starchy potato varieties such as Russet, Golden Wonder or Maris Piper.

WAFFLE-CUT CRISPS

If you have a criss-cross cutter (we use the Börner one), you can use this recipe to make waffle-cut crisps instead.

CHEESE & ONION

If you want to opt for a cheese and onion flavour, get some onion salt and sprinkle it over the cooked crisps instead of fine sea salt along with some nutritional yeast and a fine grating of firm Parmesan cheese for an outrageously OTT and visually appealing option.

USE A SPRAY BOTTLE

Where seasoning is concerned, culinary genius Heston Blumenthal demonstrated using a spray bottle to dispense the vinegar a few years ago and changed the game in our eyes. It 100% makes sense, giving a light savoury mist rather than a sharp acidic glaze over everything. Plus adding the vinegar before the salt helps the salt to adhere better. These small spray bottles are often available where you'd get the 100ml containers used for toiletries and some kitchenware shops may sell them too. For salt and vinegar crisps, simply add a few sprays or shakes of malt vinegar to your freshly fried crisps before adding the salt, as per the recipe.

GINGER BEER ONION RINGS

SERVES 4–6

We're all about levelling up flavour and texture in every recipe we share, so why settle for sparkling water or limit yourself to lager – why not reach for the sweet tang and fiery bite of ginger beer in your onion ring batter? The whole seeds and spices add another dimension to the batter, punctuating each mouthful with a fragrant hit. We love that it is like a lucky dip of which spices you might get, so play around with your favourites.

sunflower oil, for deep-frying

200g self-raising flour

2 tsp smoked sweet paprika

2 tsp black mustard seeds

2 tsp nigella seeds

1 tsp cumin seeds

½ tsp fennel seeds

1 tsp fine sea salt

¼ tsp ground white pepper

350ml fridge-cold ginger beer

75g cornflour

2–3 large white onions, cut into 1.5cm-thick rounds

Heat the oil in your deep-fryer to 180°C.

Measure the flour, paprika, seeds, salt and pepper into a large mixing bowl and whisk to combine.

Wait until the oil is up to temperature, then just before you're about to fry, whisk in the ginger beer – don't over-beat, as this will make the batter too heavy and activate the gluten too much. Whisk it just enough to make a batter about the consistency of full-fat milk.

Put the cornflour in a small baking dish or lipped plate for the first coating of the onions. Dredge each onion ring through the cornflour, shaking off the excess, then submerge each coated round in the batter before adding to the fryer.

Cook in batches (depending on the size of your fryer) for 2–3 minutes before lifting the basket, slightly shaking to drain off the excess oil, and removing to a wire rack set over a baking tray lined with kitchen paper to further drain and remain crisp. Serve while still warm, as these don't keep well and are too delicious to resist anyway.

BUFFALO FRICKLES

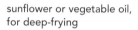

SERVES 2 AS A SNACK

Polarising at the best of times, gherkins, pickles and other members of the O'Brine family are a real love-it-or-loathe-it addition to a burger. We often think something pickled adds a freshness and sharp vibrancy to most dishes, especially when cutting through fatty richness.

But what about making pickles, usually relegated to bit part, the scene-stealing character in the spotlight just for a moment? Coated in a crisp jacket, these are a delicious snack of extremes – soft, crunchy, sharp, hot, salty and juicy in every single bite. The briny tang coupled with hot sauce is a fabulous flavour combination.

sunflower or vegetable oil, for deep-frying

3–4 whole pickles in brine

2 tbsp plain flour

1 egg

2 tbsp Buffalo wing-style hot sauce

60g fine dried breadcrumbs

1 tsp smoked sweet paprika

½ tsp cayenne pepper

TO SERVE:

blue cheese dip or extra hot sauce

Heat the oil in your deep-fryer to 170°C.

Remove your pickles from the jar and pat them dry on kitchen paper. If you don't want them whole you can slice them lengthways into 1.5cm-thick strips, but we're personally all about the full pickle.

Place the flour in one bowl. In another, whisk the egg and hot sauce together, then in a third bowl or dish, combine the breadcrumbs with the paprika and cayenne pepper.

Cover each pickle in flour, shaking off any excess, then dip into the spicy egg mix to coat and finally deep dive into the breadcrumbs. This will require a double coating for the best texture, so repeat the egg and seasoned breadcrumbs steps.

Place them all into the fryer if you have enough space and fry for around 3–4 minutes, depending on size. Drain on a wire rack set over a baking tray lined with kitchen paper and leave to cool for a further minute or two.

Serve with a blue cheese dip or extra hot sauce, depending on how much heat you can handle!

TEMPURA OYSTERS

SERVES 4–6 AS A SNACK

That shatteringly crisp tempura is truly something special when it comes to frying. Though commonly associated with Japan, did you know that the tempura technique actually originated in Portugal? It's almost unbelievable how a batter so thin, delicate and barely coaxed into being can produce such a strong statement crunch. The key here is using something carbonated and keeping it freezing cold, so we opt for sparkling water and keep it in the fridge for at least an hour before using.

Yuzu is an East Asian citrus fruit that's somewhat like a cross between a lemon, a grapefruit and a mandarin. Stirring the juice into a standard mayonnaise adds a whole other dimension, especially good when paired with seafood.

sunflower or vegetable oil, for deep-frying

40g plain flour

40g rice flour

40g cornflour, plus 30g extra for dredging

¼ tsp fine sea salt (the oysters have a natural salty-sweet flavour, so you don't need much)

⅛ tsp ground white pepper

12 oysters, shucked and flesh patted dry

150ml fridge-cold sparkling water

TO SERVE:

lemon wedges

yuzu mayonnaise

Heat the oil in your deep-fryer to 180°C.

Whisk together the plain flour, rice flour and 40g of cornflour in a mixing bowl with the salt and white pepper.

Put the remaining 30g of cornflour in a small bowl and dredge the oyster meat through it to completely coat, shaking off the excess.

Whisk the cold sparkling water into the mixing bowl until just combined into a thin batter, like a crêpe batter. Don't over-mix the batter – in fact, some small lumps are positively encouraged. Working quickly, cover the oysters one by one in the batter, then place gently into the hot oil.

Cooking in batches of four or five oysters, fry for 60–90 seconds before lifting the basket to drain, then further draining on a wire rack set over a baking tray lined with kitchen paper.

Enjoy immediately with a squeeze of lemon juice or dipped into yuzu mayonnaise.

We're lucky to live in a country so abundantly blessed with oyster production. Many areas of our rugged coast cultivate incredible oysters, like Carlingford Oysters, run by the Louët-Feisser family, local to us in County Louth. To name just a few others, you'll find Harty's Oysters in the Irish-speaking region of An Rinn in Waterford, Flaggy Shore Oysters in County Clare's picturesque Burren region, Millbay Oysters in Down, Cromane Bay Oysters in Kerry and both Kelly and DK Connemara in Galway.

TRY THIS

Reserve some of the supplementary saline juice from the shucked oysters to add to a martini.

11

BACON & CHEESE CROQUETTES WITH AIOLI

MAKES 12–15

Croquettes have got to be the most craveable tapa. Such simple joy derived from bite-sized morsels of béchamel – usually in bed with jamón and a full-flavoured cheese – encased within a barely-there jacket, yielding almost entirely to its molten middle on first impact.

While Manchego and the Basque cheese Idiazabal (our fave!) may be more traditional, we're opting for an Alpine cheese instead. Comté and Gruyère – with all their nutty, earthy, vegetal, hay barn, forest floor flavours – are perfect in croquettes and we even have some Irish equivalents. Try Teresa Roche's Kylemore cheese from east Galway or Templegall from the Hegarty family farm in County Cork.

As for the bacon, we adore something special like the offcuts of a smoked collar of bacon here, but any form of cooked ham works well, smoked if possible (note to self: add flavour at every step). Since the meat and cheese are both fairly scant in this recipe, really try to use the best you can find.

400ml full-fat milk

1 bay leaf

1 tsp whole black peppercorns

60g butter

½ medium-sized white onion, finely diced

1 garlic clove, grated

60g plain flour

70g Alpine cheese, grated (see the intro)

70g cooked ham or bacon, shredded or cut into pea-sized cubes

sunflower or vegetable oil, for deep-frying

30g plain flour

2 large eggs, whisked

100g fine dried breadcrumbs

flaky sea salt, to garnish

Put the milk, bay leaf and peppercorns in a small saucepan. Bring to the boil to infuse the milk, then strain into a jug or bowl and leave to one side.

Melt the butter in a saucepan over a low or medium-low heat. Before the butter gets too hot, add the onion and garlic and cook for around 5 minutes. You don't want them to become crispy or burn; you want them to just gently release their flavours, turn soft and translucent and begin to break down.

Add the flour, whisking to start making your roux. Cook out for about 1 minute.

Remove the pan from the heat and slowly pour in the infused milk, whisking constantly until smooth. Return the pan to the heat and add the cheese and ham as well as a generous grinding of black pepper and a little sprinkle of salt – you don't want too much salt, as the cheese and ham are already bringing that to the party.

Line a 20cm square brownie tin or a similar-sized small baking tray with parchment paper. Pour in the mixture

FOR THE AIOLI:

3 egg yolks, at room temperature

1 tbsp white wine vinegar

300ml neutral oil (such as sunflower, vegetable or grapeseed oil)

3 large garlic cloves, grated

50ml extra virgin olive oil

sea salt and freshly ground black pepper

and spread it into the corners, then cover with cling film, ensuring it directly touches the surface of the mixture to prevent a skin forming. Allow to cool fully, then leave in the fridge for at least 2 hours.

Meanwhile, to make the aioli, add the egg yolks, vinegar and 150ml of the neutral oil to a tall receptacle (we use the beaker from a NutriBullet, but you could use any tall beaker where the end of a hand-held stick blender can comfortably hit the bottom – this is very important). Allow the oil to settle on top, then put the blender down through the oil directly to the bottom of the beaker and pulse vigorously to combine – it should emulsify pretty quickly. Don't be tempted to move the blender up and down – keep the head of the blender at the bottom and the vortex will quickly bring everything together.

Pour in the remaining 150ml of oil and allow it to settle on top of the now-emulsified mixture. Put the blender down through the mixture to the bottom of the beaker again and pulse until completely emulsified. Decant to a mixing bowl, then using a hand whisk, whisk in the garlic, extra virgin olive oil and the seasoning (taste first to judge how much is needed). Keep this in a sterilised jar in the fridge for up to one week.

When you're ready to cook your croquettes, heat the oil in your deep-fryer to 160°C.

Prepare your pané station: put the flour in one bowl; in another, the beaten eggs; and in a third, the breadcrumbs.

Now it's time to shape your croquettes.

Sometimes the mixture can be quite sticky, so feel free to keep your hands wet to make this far easier. Option A is to cut the mixture into finger shapes, which usually yields about 12, or Option B, you can use a heaped teaspoon and roll it into a ball instead.

Place each shaped croquette into the flour first, giving it an even coating, followed by the egg and then the breadcrumbs. Pop into the fryer and cook for 2–3 minutes, until they are golden brown. If they peek over the oil line, use a slotted spoon to move them around to colour evenly. However, avoid shaking the basket excessively while they fry – they are delicate and this runs the risk of them bursting.

Shake the basket to remove the excess oil, then tip out onto on a wire rack set over a baking tray lined with kitchen paper to cool for a few moments. Sprinkle some flaky sea salt on top and serve with the aioli.

ALL ABOUT AIOLI

Aioli is the perfect accompaniment to dip the croquettes into. The traditional Catalan name *allioli* gives away the two key ingredients: *all* (garlic) and *oli* (oil). This was originally just garlic and oil bashed together to a paste, but the egg yolks add stability and structure to the thick dip we now know as aioli. You could make this a saffron aioli by adding a small pinch of saffron threads into the beaker at the beginning.

TRY THESE

TRY THESE
CROQUETTE FILLINGS

This is not *THE* croqueta recipe, it's just a base to begin from, so change up the fillings to suit yourself.

SLOW-COOKED

Any kind of slow-cooked or pulled meat like pulled pork, lamb, chicken or duck would work well.

CRABBY

Crab also works wonderfully, maybe with some sweetcorn and finely chopped spring onions.

CHEESY

Why not amp up the cheese for a three-cheese version? Add some hard Cheddar and blue cheese to go alongside the Alpine cheese in lieu of ham.

SESAME PRAWN TOASTS

SERVES 4–6 (MAKES 24 TRIANGLES)

Hong Kong captivated us on our travels there a couple of years ago and still has a special place in our hearts. This Cantonese dim sum snack bore a cutting-edge, East-meets-West combination of flavoured prawn paste and plain ol' white bread when it was first introduced. However simple it may seem, something magical happens in the fusion of these two key ingredients when introduced to hot oil – even more so in our part of the world, where the prawn paste is liberally coated with sesame seeds to add a crunchy topping. This little appetiser has become ubiquitous in Chinese restaurants in Ireland and the UK. Crisp, sweet, salty, crunchy; so satisfying.

neutral oil (such as sunflower, vegetable or grapeseed), for deep-frying

300g raw prawns, peeled and deveined

20g fresh ginger, peeled and finely chopped

2–3 garlic cloves, finely chopped

1–2 fresh red chillies, deseeded and finely chopped

1 large egg white

1 tbsp sesame oil

1 tbsp light soy sauce

1 tsp fine sea salt

1 tsp ground white pepper

1 tsp Chinese black or white rice vinegar (optional)

75g white sesame seeds

2 tbsp black sesame seeds (optional)

6 large slices of white bread (crusts off or on)

Heat the oil in your deep-fryer to 180°C. Alternatively, if you're using a high-sided saucepan or pot, heat about 4cm of oil on a medium-high heat. You'll know it has come up to temperature when a small piece of bread dropped in the hot oil instantly floats and is surrounded by medium-sized bubbles.

Combine 225g of the prawns with the ginger, garlic, red chillies, egg white, sesame oil, soy sauce, salt, pepper and vinegar (if using) in a food processor and blitz briefly to a paste. Take care not to make it so fine that it gets watery – pulse just until the prawns have broken down but the mixture still holds its shape, not dissimilar to a fish pâté. Decant to a mixing bowl.

Take the remaining 75g of prawns and chop by hand into small pieces, then stir them through the paste to add a gorgeous chunky texture.

Spread out the sesame seeds in a lipped bowl or dish. Stack the slices of bread on a chopping board and cut through so that each piece is split into four even-sized triangles, corner to opposite corner.

Take a triangle of bread and spread roughly 1 tablespoon of the prawn paste from the middle out to each corner using a spoon or dinner knife. At each corner, curve the mixture slightly downwards so that it ends seamlessly

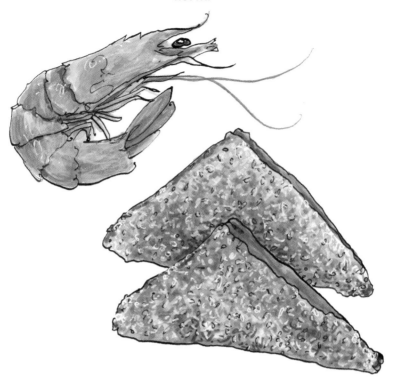

TO SERVE:

spicy chilli, sweet and sour
or plum sauce

at the edge rather than leaving it jagged and exposed. Repeat with each triangle of bread and put them spaced apart on a baking tray or clean board.

When you're ready to fry (and happy with the oil's temperature), take each triangle and turn it prawn side down into the sesame seeds, pressing lightly to coat the entire top. Place immediately, sesame and prawn side down, into the hot oil. Cook in batches, depending on how many you can comfortably fit in your fryer without overcrowding them, for 2 minutes on the prawn side, then flip over and cook for a further 90 seconds on the bread side, until light golden. Drain and remove to a wire rack set over a baking tray lined with kitchen paper to absorb any excess oil. Repeat with all remaining pieces.

Serve while still warm, either on their own or dipped into an accompanying sauce like a spicy chilli, sweet and sour or plum sauce.

BLACK PUDDING SCOTCH EGGS

MAKES 2

We have a habit of including black pudding in a wide array of recipes – as many as possible, really. We just adore it as a diverse ingredient, not least because Ireland boasts some of the finest BPs around, from Tipperary's Inch House and Annascaul in Kerry to McCarthy's of Kanturk and the ever-iconic Clonakilty, both from Cork. Use your favourite or opt for your local butcher's unique iteration. To bring this to another level, we suggest seeking out Hugh Maguire's 'The Smokin' Butcher' Beechwood Smoked Black Pudding. Not only was it awarded three stars at the prestigious Great Taste Awards, but this product also clinched the overall Supreme Champion gong in 2017.

3 medium eggs

sunflower or vegetable oil, for deep-frying

150g sausage meat

100g black pudding

50g plain flour

flaky sea salt and freshly ground black pepper

75g panko breadcrumbs

TO SERVE:

mustard

piccalilli or chutney

dressed green leaves

Soft-boil two of the eggs by bringing a pot of water to the boil, then placing two eggs into it and cooking for 5 minutes to ensure runny yolks. Ready yourself with a bowl of iced water and transfer your eggs directly into it to stop the cooking and retain the desired yolk consistency. Leave to cool.

Heat the oil in your deep-fryer to 170°C. Because of the oval shape and the size of the eggs, try to ensure you are hitting the maximum limit line for the oil.

If necessary, remove and discard the casing from your sausages and black pudding. Place the meat in a bowl, then use a clean hand mix it all together until the sausage meat and black pudding have basically fused into one.

Prepare your pané station with three separate wide, shallow dishes: one for beating the remaining egg, another for the flour (stir through a little seasoning) and the third for the panko breadcrumbs.

Carefully remove the shells of the soft-boiled eggs by gently cracking them off a hard surface and peeling under a running tap. Return to the bowl of cold water until ready to shape.

Get a large square of cling film and spread half of the sausage–pudding mix on it in an even layer roughly

25cm square. Place your peeled egg in the middle, then pull the corners of the cling film together to gently and evenly wrap the egg in the meat. Take your time to be precise here.

Now cover the meat-wrapped egg evenly in flour, then submerge quickly into the beaten egg before generously coating in the panko.

Deep-fry in the hot oil for 7–8 minutes, until golden in colour, turning each egg every couple of minutes to ensure they cook evenly. Drain and place on a wire rack set over a baking tray lined with kitchen paper to absorb any excess oil, then season with flaky sea salt.

To serve, cut in half and enjoy with a bit of fiery mustard, a dollop of sharp piccalilli or chutney and some dressed green leaves.

A SHORT HISTORY OF THE SCOTCH EGG

Though the 'Scotch' in the title may seem to suggest this is a Scottish invention, there's actually no Scottish connection to this handheld snack. The Scotch egg is believed to have been created in the seaside Yorkshire town of Whitby and named after the surname, Scot, of the inventor. The UK being at one time a vast and expansive empire, there is also a suggestion that this snack isn't actually British in origin at all, with some pointing out similarities to historic dishes in both India and North Africa. How and ever, it was the London-based purveyor of fine foods, Fortnum & Mason on Piccadilly, that popularised this grab-and-go snack for those on the move in the 1700s, so think more horse and cart rather than Jubilee Line.

Growing in wider popularity through the 18th and 19th centuries, variations of the Scotch egg began to be documented, notably by writers like Maria Rundell and Mrs Beeton. Fast forward to today and the Scotch egg shows no sign of its popularity or presence waning, running the gamut from bite-sized canapé versions using quail eggs to vegetarian varieties replacing the sausage meat with potato or pulses. For us, the addition of black pudding adds that next level of deliciousness – and heightens our personal joy at being able to include one of our favourite ingredients in a recipe.

LASAGNE BITES

MAKES 6–8

You may think we've gone down a weird path with this one, but hear us out! Cookbooks can have this compulsion to instruct you to make everything from scratch, but sometimes convenience needs to be encouraged to get the job done. So be kind to yourself and take the easy route here. Pop into the supermarket and get your paws on the best ready-made lasagne you can find, then you're going to create culinary magic by portioning it up and deep-frying it. Think mac 'n' cheese bites, but better. Think oozy, creamy, rich lasagne but hand-held and crunchy. The ideal little bar snack, indulgent treat or crowd-pleasing canapé, we bet you never thought lasagne could be this lavish!

1 ready-made beef lasagne (about 400g)

sunflower or vegetable oil, for deep-frying

2 tbsp plain flour

1 large egg

1 tbsp milk

50g panko breadcrumbs (or fine dried breadcrumbs)

10g freshly grated Parmesan, Grana Padano or Pecorino cheese

flaky sea salt and freshly cracked black pepper

Get your pre-made lasagne from the supermarket. Remove the cling film or other wrapping, but with the lasagne still in its foil tray, use a sharp knife to cut it into roughly 4cm squares, as if it's a sort of traybake. A 400g lasagne will yield around six nuggets, while a larger one may get you eight to 10. Cover the tray with a sheet of cling film and place in the freezer for about 90 minutes to 2 hours to solidify a bit.

Heat the oil in your deep-fryer to 160°C.

Prepare your pané station: put your flour in one bowl. In another, whisk the egg and milk together. In a third, combine the breadcrumbs with the cheese and some freshly cracked black pepper. (You would sprinkle, grate or twist these over a finished pasta dish, right? So why not include them in the coating?)

Take the now semi-frozen lasagne out of the freezer and carefully remove the pre-cut cubes. One by one, place each lasagne bite into the flour, then into the egg, covering all six sides. Smother in the breadcrumbs and cheese, then return it into the egg, and again into the breadcrumbs. The double coating ensures there shouldn't be any leaks.

Working in batches, gently lower into the fryer, shaking the basket slightly to ensure it doesn't stick. Fry for 8–10 minutes, depending on the thickness of your lasagne. If a little protrudes out of the top, don't worry. You'll have to turn them around about every 2 minutes to ensure even coverage.

Remove from the fryer and place on a wire rack set over a baking tray lined with kitchen paper to absorb any excess oil. Leave to stand for about 2 minutes, as they will still be molten inside! Season with a little flaky sea salt and black pepper on top before serving.

AN ODE TO CHIPS

More often than not the deep-fryer is associated with chips – so much so that we've popped a cornet of pommes frites on this book's cover, and with good reason. While *Hot Fat* aims to bring that narrative of frying in hot oil along and demonstrate dizzying delicious possibilities beyond chips, it would be remiss of us to overlook one of life's greatest pleasures: the chip. It's the carbohydrate equivalent of a cup of tea when you find yourself in desperate need of edible comfort and self-care satisfaction.

Chips, frites, fries – whatever you call them, chips are an inseparable partner to fried fish with a tartare sidekick and what cheeseburger is complete without fries and a shake, soda or beer? However, we find chips to be perfection set centre stage and solo; edible nirvana when eaten fresh from the fat and adorned with a generous dollop of sauce…

You see, for us, Belgium sits at the epicentre of the chip world, and we follow the Belgian way of eating them. There's scarcely a more perfect, pure eating experience than savouring a cornet of sauce-adorned frites on a terrace in Brussels with a beer in hand, surrounded by strangers speaking different languages but all enjoying, understanding and cherishing the same thing: the unrivalled majesty of simple fried sticks of potato. Within Brussels alone, the opportunity exists to indulge like nowhere else on a chip pilgrimage.

Without starting a chip-flinging conflict between neighbouring nations, France and Belgium have an ongoing, often fraught and impassioned debate about who began the phenomenon of fried potato sticks. The expression 'French fries' is sometimes traced back to US President Thomas Jefferson, who enjoyed 'potatoes served in the French manner', and Pont Neuf in Paris is indeed documented as a selling point for fried potatoes in the late 18th century. Others say it came later, attributed to American soldiers stationed in French-speaking areas of Belgium during World War One. However, to give the last word to the president of the Belgian association of friture/frituur (fritkot owners): 'If frites came from France, there would be friteries all over France, but there aren't.' We tend to agree.

We could write a thesis on chips (stop encouraging us!), but on these pages we want to convey and conjure the magic of the chip. The French (Belgian) fry. Pommes frites.

There are four things that most Belgian friteries note as the key to fried potato success: double frying at two different temperatures; cooking in beef dripping; choosing the right potato variety; and tossing the freshly fried frites in the air in stainless steel mixing bowls to bring down the temperature, add an even seasoning and ward off the sogginess that can occur when chips sit tightly packed.

Where is our favourite fritkot? Set in the heart of Brussels's EU quarter is Maison Antoine, regarded by many as the best in Brussels. Founded by Antoine Desmet in a shack on Place Jourdan left behind by the German army in 1948, it's an unlikely and unusual spot for one of the most enduring and popular purveyors of frites in the city. Don't be shocked to find a queue over an hour long at peak times. Handily, many bars on Place Jourdan display signs showing a cornet of frites, meaning hey, you're more than welcome to appoint yourself on one of our terrace tables to enjoy your fries as long as you buy a drink.

OUR FAVOURITE PLACES IN BELGIUM FOR FRITES

Maison Antoine: Probably the longest-running and most-beloved fritkot in the city, known to attract a lot of high-profile EU officials.

Fritkot Flagey: Appointed on Place Flagey near the former broadcasting building-turned-cultural arts centre, try something from their huge list of sauces.

Friterie Tabora: Set on its namesake street between Boulevard Anspach and Grand Place, this is probably the best (and smallest) in the city centre, with sauces chaudes options too. Don't even try to resist the waffles from Los Churros next door.

Frieterij: In the Berchem district of Antwerp on Boomgaardstraat, Frieterij takes a more health-conscious approach with less oil and more pronounced potato-flavoured chips, served on fancy trays.

Frites Atelier: What luxury couture is to fashion, these are to frites. Born in Amsterdam from chef Sergio Herman and now with outposts in Den Haag, Brussels, Antwerp and Ghent, this is the lavish, premium, ultra-indulgent approach to frites, restaurant-style.

Frituur Tartaar: A hipster frites bar in historic Ghent, where the tartare is made fresh daily and as much as possible is local and artisanal.

CONDIMENTS

To channel our inner Joan Rivers, 'Can we talk?' People have this thing about Polish *majonez*, finding it tangier, sharper, sweeter and creamier than your standardly ubiquitous Hellmann's. Others may only have eyes for Japanese Kewpie and we have our own grá for the smoked onion mayo made by Heather Flaherty at Builín Blasta café in An Spidéal, County Galway. In Belgium, they're crazy about condiments with their chips and their own mayonnaise reigns supreme. Two or three pumps from big tubs of the stuff adorn each cornet, complete with a dinky coloured plastic fork speared atop the highest chip.

Where mayonnaise (and to a lesser extent ketchup) may be foremost favoured, this hits home at an integral element of the experience of enjoying Belgian frites: the dizzying variety of sauces available, one for everyone in the audience! Often a board will display which sauces are available. Most are usually cold, pre-made and mayonnaise-based, and you'll almost always find some form of tartare, cocktail and pepper sauces. But sometimes sauces chaudes (hot sauces) take the form of carbonnade (Flemish stew), satay, fromage (cheese) or champignon (mushroom) lavished piping hot over the top of the frites.

Try these sauces next time you're eating frites in Belgium:

- Sweet pepper-piqued andalouse
- Lightly spicy samouraï
- Garlic and herby pita
- Piccalilli-like pickels
- Fruity, tangy Brasil
- Mammouth, which is like an onion-rich dopiaza
- Americaine, kind of a Bruxellois twist on burger sauce

ALL POTATOES ARE NOT CREATED EQUAL

Picking potato varieties for chips can be tricky, as not all potatoes create great chips. In Belgium, a variety called Bintje (which are grown plentifully around Benelux) is most widely used. In fact, many outlets here in Ireland order in these premium chipping potatoes, but the general public will struggle to find them in the supermarket. Your best options are the lesser-spotted Russet (very popular among fry fans in the US), while Maris Piper is Miss Congeniality in our part of the world, the ultimate all-rounder for perfect chips. Kerr's Pinks, when in their seasonal prime, also give a shatteringly crisp texture when fried. It's the sugar (carbohydrate) content that dictates how crisp and golden-coloured a chip is when deep-fried, and this varies wildly not only between potato varieties but also from farm to farm, shop to shop and season to season.

It's important to remember that a potato is a cool weather vegetable crop and that, naturally, it has a season. A season starts and a season ends, then you wait patiently for the season to start again. Potatoes are planted in late winter or early spring, then harvested between summer and autumn, running from earlies to main crop. When not packed for sale, they're often already plucked out of the ground and kept stacked in tonne boxes in dark, cold warehouses to ensure year-round supply, unless otherwise imported. Let's remind ourselves that access to potatoes year-round is actually an odd phenomenon.

A note: the potato has more in common with a tomato or an aubergine (eggplant) than a sweet potato. The sweet potato hails from the fabulously camp-sounding Morning Glory family (*Convolvulaceae*), whereas the regular potato belongs to the nightshade (*Solanaceae*) family of plants. Though both commonly known as tubers, potatoes are stem tubers and sweet potatoes are root tubers. Judging by their appearance you might think that they're sisters, but they're actually quite distant, even estranged, cousins. Sweet potatoes were first cultivated around the Yucatán peninsula in Mexico by the Caribbean Sea, but potatoes actually hail from the opposite side of South America, around the border between Peru and Bolivia. In fact, of the 5,000+ varieties of potato in the world today, roughly 3,000 are found in the Andes region of South America alone. Let's not even get started on yams…

A WORD ON FAT

Fat = flavour, and while we adore nothing more than beef dripping fries – and we are never without brick-shaped blocks of James Whelan Butcher's award-winning beef dripping in our fridge – it's not recommended to use in most domestic deep-fryers. It can harden around the heating element and cause issues unless you dispose of the oil while it's still liquid, but cleaning off leftover dripping is also a nightmare. As quickly as dripping melts, it almost as quickly cools and solidifies again, so if you want to use dripping for chips, we suggest a heavy-based saucepan with a thermometer and then follow the recipe on the next page. It's far easier to remove the dripping from the pan once you're done, and if you're just using that same dripping for chips, you'll get a handful of batches from it.

THE DOUBLE FRY

The double fry is essential in our book, but we also add in a small extra step beforehand: parboiling the chips for a couple of minutes in salted water, then draining and cooling them. Another tip, which you may already do with roast potatoes, is to add some extra texture to the parboiled and drained potatoes by sprinkling them with flour just before frying. Texture is *everything* and chips are no exception, so try it out.

OUR PERFECT CHIPS

While chips are beautiful on their own, you can use them as a base for many other dishes: chip kebabs, gyros, taco fries, poutine, chip butties, masala chips, moules-frites, disco fries ...

1½ potatoes per person (floury varieties, such as Maris Piper or Russett)

sunflower or vegetable oil, for deep-frying

2 tbsp plain flour

malt vinegar

fine sea salt

Cut your potatoes into batons about 7cm long and 1.5cm wide, but there's no need to get out the ruler here – chips should be a joy, not a chore. Skin on or off, that's your preference, but ideally keep the skin only for those potato varieties with thinner skins.

Soak the batons in cold water for at least 5 minutes, but you can leave them to soak for an hour or two if making ahead.

When it's time to cook, parboil the batons first by bringing a pot of salted water to the boil, then add the potatoes and cook for 3–4 minutes. It's important that they maintain their shape and not become mushy. Drain them in a colander, then sprinkle over the flour while still in the colander, shaking gently to cover and coat.

Heat the oil in your deep-fryer to 160°C. When the oil has come up to temperature, fry the chips in batches (don't overload the fryer!) for about 5 minutes per batch. This is a lower temperature for the first fry.

Remove, drain directly on kitchen paper and leave to cool down slightly. After all the batches have had their first fry, crank up the temperature of the oil to 190°C.

Fry all the chips (again, in batches if need be) for another 90 seconds to 2 minutes. During this higher-temperature fry they will crisp up and turn golden, but this process is quick so keep an eye on them. Drain using the basket, then remove to a metal mixing bowl, shaking them up in the air (as the Belgians do!) to firm up that crisp exterior and cool them down.

Finally, spray with vinegar and sprinkle over some fine sea salt. Do it in this order as the vinegar is wet, helping the salt to stick.

HASH BROWNS

MAKES 6–8

Hash browns, latkes, röstis – all fried potato-based beauties. A hash brown is never far from our fryer, whether the homemade variety, such as these, or in case of frequent emergency hanger pangs, a box from the supermarket. As a make-ahead recipe, these are a dream – you can cook them fresh or store them in the freezer raw for when you need them. The fresh ones are extra crisp and sublimely scraggly, similar to aloo bhaji but without the spice.

2–3 medium white potatoes, such as Golden Wonder, Maris Piper or Mayan Gold (approx. 400–500g), peeled

1 tsp fine sea salt

sunflower or vegetable oil, for deep-frying

2–3 spring onions, thinly sliced

a handful of chopped fresh chives (optional)

1 tsp freshly cracked black pepper

1 large egg, beaten

40g cornflour

flaky sea salt, for sprinkling

Using the coarse side of a box grater, grate your potatoes into a mixing bowl. Sprinkle over ½ teaspoon of the salt and using a wooden spoon or your hands, give it a good mix. You'll start to see the starchy water leaching out from the potatoes. Keep squelching and squeezing all the liquid out and discard it. You could use a clean tea towel to squeeze it all out if you like. Continue until there is little to no liquid left.

Heat the oil in your deep-fryer to 170°C.

Add the spring onions, chives (if using), the remaining ½ teaspoon of salt and the freshly cracked black pepper to the grated potato in the mixing bowl. Stir in the egg followed by the cornflour until everything is incorporated.

Using slightly wet hands, form into patties roughly the size of your palm, flattening slightly. An oval shape works, but you can shape into squares, triangles or circles if you prefer. This mixture makes enough for six to eight hash browns, each weighing about 50–55g (or a dessertspoon amount).

Working in batches, place into the hot oil, being careful of splashes, and fry for 4 minutes, turning each one at least once. Don't allow these to become too golden. Place on a wire rack set over a baking tray lined with kitchen paper to absorb any excess oil and sprinkle with some flaky sea salt. Best served with eggs and bacon, and sometimes with the stain of last night's red wine still on your lips. We personally consider hash browns to cure and comfort in equal measure, 110% of the time.

HOW TO
FREEZE HASH BROWNS

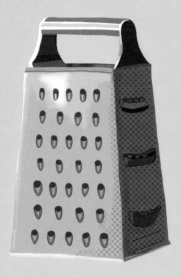

If you're freezing the raw hash browns, shape them and place on a flat plate or board lined with parchment paper, then pop into the freezer for a minimum of 1 hour. If leaving longer, once frozen individually keep them together in a freezerproof ziplock bag. To cook, heat the oil in your deep-fryer to 160°C and fry for 5 minutes, until cooked on the inside and golden on the outside. Straight from the freezer, you need a longer cook time and a slightly lower temperature than when cooking them fresh.

POTATO PAVÉ

SERVES 2–4

If you think the rest of this book is indulgent, please take a seat and allow us to introduce you to our potato pavé. This is something special. It takes a bit of work, a bit of time and a bit of patience, but what you ultimately get is a crispy fried potato gratin and honestly, who doesn't love the comfort of a gratin?

The ideal equipment to make this in is a dish you have two of and can stack. A 20cm square brownie tin is ideal, but two loaf tins can work too. Failing that, cut out a square of cardboard the same size as the top of your tin and cover it with a few layers of tin foil – weighing it down is important to compress those iconic layers.

150ml double cream

1 large garlic clove, finely chopped

flaky sea salt and freshly ground black pepper

3–4 large white potatoes (such as Golden Wonder, Maris Piper or Mayan Gold), peeled

50g butter, diced into very small chunks, at room temperature, plus extra for greasing (or oil)

sunflower or vegetable oil, for deep-frying, plus extra for greasing

chopped fresh chives, to garnish

Preheat the oven to 180°C.

Place the cream, garlic and some salt and pepper in a large bowl and stir together.

Using a mandolin or a very sharp knife, cut the potatoes into thin slices about 2–3mm thick. You don't want transparent potato slices, so be mindful of how thin they are. Place the potatoes into the cream.

Grease the dish or tin you're using with butter or oil and line with parchment paper, leaving a considerable overhang on each side as you'll eventually fold the paper sides over the top of the dish.

Begin to build up the layers by taking slice after slice of potato and placing it into the dish. Uniformity is key, so lay every slice down in the same shape and orientation. After every second or third layer, throw a few small chunks of butter on top and repeat until the dish is filled just above three-quarters of the way up the tin. Discard any cream that's left over.

Wrap the parchment paper over the top, then cover the top of the tin with foil. Bake in the oven for 80–100 minutes. You'll know it's done when you poke a skewer into it and it doesn't feel in any way solid. Remove from the oven, discard the foil and allow to cool for about 30 minutes.

Now weigh the potatoes down. As mentioned in the intro, if you have two tins that slot into each other, happy days. If not, use the cardboard and foil method from the intro and place it on top. Use some tins to weigh down the potatoes. There may be a slight seepage of cream, so just be careful. Leave it like this on the counter for another half hour or so.

Place this into the fridge for a minimum of 2 hours, still weighed down with the tins, but it's better to leave it overnight.

When it's time to fry, heat the oil in your deep-fryer or a high-sided pan to 170°C.

While this works very well in the fryer, it is suitable to pan-fry in a smaller quantity of oil too. The issue with pan-frying, though, is the constant turning, while the fryer submerges it evenly in the oil. If you do pan-fry, we recommend using beef dripping with some fresh rosemary and a crushed garlic clove in there for added flavour.

Remove the pavé from the fridge and allow it to come to room temperature for around 15 minutes. Peel the parchment paper off the top to expose it completely. Place a chopping board on top, then invert it (like a tarte tatin) and tip the wrapped pavé out of the tin, peeling off all the paper and unveiling what is essentially a solid potato gratin. Tidy it up by cutting off the sides to reveal one perfect rectangle with all the layers exposed. This should make 10–12 cubes about 4cm x 4cm each or you can do longer finger-shaped slices.

Working in batches, place the cubes or slices into the fryer basket and cook for about 4 minutes in total. If pan-frying, you'll need to turn the pieces regularly so that they are evenly fried on all sides.

Place the finished cubes or slices on some kitchen paper to absorb any excess oil. Top with cracked black pepper, a sprinkling of flaky sea salt and chopped chives.

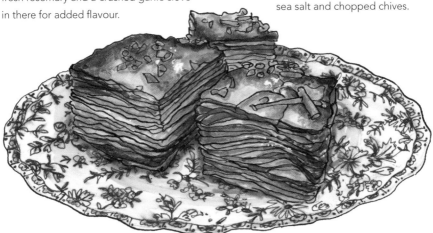

FISH FILLET BURGERS

MAKES 4

If you love a fish fillet burger from a certain pair of golden arches, did you know that most of the time you have to wait for them as they have to cook them to order? However, we're here to tell you that a homemade version is even better than the original. So fresh, full of flavour and easily achievable at home – you'll be amazed at how well this turns out, and yes, processed cheese slices are positively decreed here. We won't be told differently.

400g fresh white fish fillets (we love hake here, but you could use haddock, whiting or ling), skinned and deboned

sea salt and freshly ground black pepper

sunflower or vegetable oil, for deep-frying

25g plain flour (roughly 3 tbsp)

1 large egg, beaten

35g panko breadcrumbs

15g fine breadcrumbs (either fresh or dried)

4 processed square cheese slices

4 brioche buns

TO SERVE:

tartare sauce (see the tip on page 36)

shredded lettuce (optional)

white onion (optional)

Preheat the oven to 180°C.

Place your fish in a baking dish and season generously with sea salt and a crack of freshly ground black pepper. Bake in the oven for 10 minutes, then remove and allow to cool completely in the dish.

Take four circular or square tart tins (ideally approx. 9cm in diameter to create the perfect shape) and line each one with cling film, making sure you leave some overhanging.

Using two forks, gently flake the cooked fish (use this opportunity to also search for any errant bones), then pack it into the lined tins, pressing down firmly. Alternatively, you could free style this if you don't have suitable tins and just shape the fish into four rough circles or squares on four separate pieces of cling film.

Cover tightly with the cling film overhang and freeze until solid (about 2–3 hours). You can leave these in the freezer for longer though and continue with the next steps when you're ready.

Heat the oil in your deep-fryer to 160°C. Take the frozen fish burgers out of the freezer.

Prepare your pané station with three separate wide, shallow dishes: one for the flour with a little seasoning added to it, another for the beaten egg and the third for a combined mixture of the panko and fine breadcrumbs.

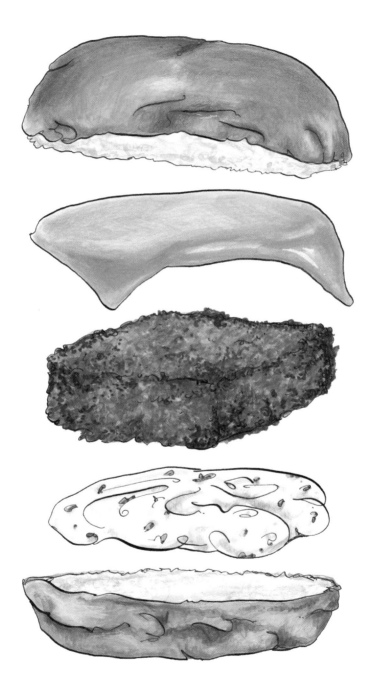

Take a frozen fish patty (which should be firm and holding its shape) and dredge it through the flour, shaking off any excess, then dunk it in the beaten egg to coat. Finally, bathe it in its breadcrumb bath, ensuring it emerges in an even coating.

Working with one burger at a time or in batches depending on the size of your fryer basket, place each burger into the basket, gently lower it into the hot oil and fry for approximately 5 minutes. Lift the basket up from the oil and allow to drain as you crank the fryer up to 190°C.

When the oil has come up to temperature, lower the fish burger into the oil for a second fry for only 60 to 90 seconds to ensure a glorious even golden brown and crisp exterior. Place on a wire rack set over a baking tray lined with kitchen paper to absorb any excess oil and top each burger with a square of the cheese while it's still piping hot.

To assemble, lightly grill or gently toast the burger buns. Spread a generous tablespoon or two of tartare sauce on the base bun, top with the still-warm cheese-crowned fish burger (and some shredded iceberg lettuce and finely diced or sliced white onion if you like) and follow with the bun lid. Savour immediately. You may even pine for a second burger – we always do.

TRY THIS

To make your own chunky tartare sauce, mix some diced gherkins and capers with some mayonnaise and a bit of lemon juice, then taste for seasoning. Add some dill or fennel fronds if you like.

HOW OFTEN SHOULD I
CHANGE THE OIL?

This is such a common question and the answer is: it depends. The more times a quantity of oil is used and heated close to or even beyond its smoke point, the more it oxidises, and eventually it can create nasty compounds – you'll see the oil take on a deeper colour and more intense scent every time.

So best practice before explaining anything else: clean your machine and store your oil correctly. Wait until your oil has cooled, then filter or drain it into a suitable receptacle (we usually use the drum or bottle it came in) and store it in a dark cupboard. Clean the fryer basin by removing any particles or residue, then wash it in warm soapy water and dry (try to choose a fryer that has a removable basin). Get into this habit of cool-drain-store-wash-dry after every time you fry.

For all our home cooking, we have used a Tefal Oleoclean deep-fryer (available in a 2- or 3-litre capacity). This fryer filters the oil out of the main tub into a box underneath, ensuring it's kept clean and that the smell doesn't linger.

So how often can you use the same oil? Well, if you're using it for the same type of thing (tempura vegetables, chips, doughnuts) and not deviating from that, maybe five or six times or even up to eight to 10 times. However, if you're often changing up what you're frying, we suggest that after using the same oil two or three times, it's time to change it. Think about it: would you like your sugared doughnuts to have the faint flavour of the sesame prawn toast from two weeks ago?

Think about what you're using your oil for and act appropriately. Are you frying something with strong odours, like onions or fish? Does what you're frying have a heavy floury coating or loose batter? Are there lots of spices, seeds, herbs or sugar that might get lost in the frying process? Use your own judgement in terms of what's being immersed in the oil. If you're ever deep-frying anything sweet, we recommend that you start on fresh (new) oil.

SQUID INK & STOUT BATTERED HAKE

MAKES 4

Beer-battered fish is so popular, but it can be confusing as to which beer styles give the best results. Likewise, how cold should the batter be? Can I make it ahead of time? What fish is best (and easiest) to use? That iconic double act of fish 'n' chips is a match made in comfort food heaven and we're staying true to our Irish roots here by suggesting you use the deep, rich flavour of stout in your batter. Not only does it add that signature beer batter flavour and crunch, but it also does double duty by adding its midnight-black hue to the batter, which is also imbued with squid ink. If you were to use water here it would come out a bland, not-so-appetising greige, so using stout and squid ink results in a seriously dramatic batter, perfectly juxtaposed with the pristine white flesh within.

sunflower or vegetable oil, for deep-frying

120g plain flour

2 tsp fine sea salt, plus extra to season

½ tsp ground white pepper

75g cornflour, split between two wide, shallow dishes

150ml fridge-cold Guinness or stout

1 x 4g sachet of squid ink (available to order from good fishmongers)

4 hake fillets (ling, haddock or whiting are also perfect here), skinned

TO SERVE:

flaky sea salt

lemon wedges or malt vinegar

Heat the oil in your deep-fryer to 175°C.

Whisk together the flour, salt and white pepper in a wide, shallow bowl.

Assemble your pané station: one wide, shallow dish with half of the cornflour, then the dish with your flour mixture, then another wide, shallow dish with the rest of the cornflour. You're going to double coat the fish, so the batter should be in the middle of the two separate dishes of cornflour as it will be used twice.

Whisk three-quarters of the stout and the sachet of squid ink into the dish of flour that's in the middle, mixing it until just combined to a batter – don't over-beat. You want to achieve the consistency of double cream, so depending on your flour you might not need all the stout or you may need more. Remember, you can always add more liquid but you can't take it out. Adding liquid activates the gluten in the flour, so only whisk it in when you're ready to fry.

Pat the fish dry and season with salt. Working with one fillet at a time, dredge it in the first dish of cornflour, patting off the excess with your left hand, then drop it into the batter, using your right hand to turn it until completely coated.

Add to the next dish of cornflour and using your 'dry' left hand again, cover it once more in cornflour before returning to the batter. Quickly but gently introduce to the hot oil, giving the basket a bit of a rigorous shake to ensure it doesn't stick.

Fry each fillet for 2–3 minutes, then drain in the basket before removing to a wire rack set over a baking tray lined with kitchen paper to further drain and rest for 60 seconds. Season with flaky sea salt and a little lemon juice or malt vinegar and serve warm.

CORN DOGS

MAKES 6 LARGE OR 12 SMALL

Which came first, the (hush) puppy or the (corn) dog? It's a bit of a chicken and egg situation that has lots of folklore-fuelled beginnings around the very early 20th century and is almost certainly apropos of African-American cooks of the Deep South. At any rate, the lil' puppies found a friend in a frankfurter and the two have been inseparable ever since. A fairground favourite in the States, the corn dog consists of a hot dog speared on a stick, dipped in a thick cornmeal batter and fried until golden with a signature fluffy interior beneath its crisp jacket. In Australia they call these Dagwood Dogs (or Dippy Dogs), where they dip the whole thing post-fryer into ketchup, rather than the more popular Stateside serve of an alternating two-tone drizzle of ketchup and yellow mustard. A note on cornflour vs: cornstarch: in the UK, cornflour refers to the thickening agent that's called cornstarch in the US.

sunflower or vegetable oil, for deep-frying

120g fine cornmeal

80g plain flour

1 large egg

175ml buttermilk

½ tsp fine sea salt

½ tsp caster sugar

¼ tsp paprika

¼ tsp ground white pepper

¼ tsp garlic powder (optional)

¼ tsp baking soda

6–8 large skinny frankfurter-style sausages and 6–8 skewers

a small dish of cornflour (cornstarch), to coat

TO SERVE:

ketchup

yellow mustard

Heat the oil in your deep-fryer to 180°C.

Prepare your batter by adding the cornmeal, flour, egg, buttermilk, salt, sugar, paprika, white pepper, garlic powder (if using) and baking soda into a mixing bowl and whisking vigorously to combine, then transfer to a tall glass, measuring jug or big NutriBullet beaker, any of which provide the height that enables enviably easy dippage to completely coat the dogs.

Pat the hot dogs dry on kitchen paper. If making small corn dogs, cut each one in half to make two, but if making large ones, just keep them whole. Skewer each one with a wooden or bamboo skewer three-quarters of the way up through the centre, taking care not to veer off and tear through the side.

Put the cornflour in a wide, shallow dish or tray, then dredge each of the sausages through it, coating completely and shaking off any excess – this helps the cornmeal batter to stick. Set aside on a plate, ready for dipping.

When ready to dip and coat, holding the wooden skewer, submerge each sausage head-first into the batter, twisting gently to coax the batter to stick, then gently and slowly

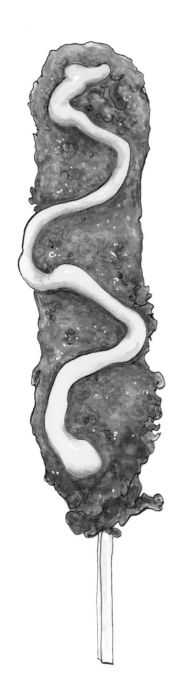

twisting as you pull the skewer up and out of the glass or jug to reveal a completely coated corn dog.

Working quickly, gently lower the battered corn dog head first into the hot oil (rather than into the fryer basket, which should already be submerged), hovering the top in the oil for a little bit to get it accustomed and then lowering it in. At this point, give the submerged basket a rigorous shake to ensure the newly arrived corn dog doesn't stick to the bottom.

Repeat this process as you fry in batches of two to four, depending on the size of your fryer, for 3–4 minutes in total. About two-thirds of the way through the cooking time, you may want to use tongs to turn the corn dogs gently to ensure they colour evenly.

When the corn dogs are an even golden colour you'll know they're done, so lift them out one by one or together in the basket, drip-draining any excess oil. Allow to further drain and cool on a wire rack set over a baking tray lined with kitchen paper as you continue with the next ones.

Enjoy immediately with ketchup and yellow mustard, your choice of condiments or just as is.

If you'd prefer to make hush puppies (and please your vegetarian pals!), we suggest upping the quantity of both cornmeal and flour by 50g each and stirring a small 200g tin of sweetcorn (drained) through the batter for extra texture. A very finely chopped spring onion wouldn't go amiss in that mixture too for a little allium kick if you don't mind the green speckles through these gorgeous blonde bites. Drop generous tablespoonfuls of the batter into the hot oil (at 180°C) and fry until lightly golden, turning once during frying.

SPICE BURGERS

MAKES 4

Born in the 1950s, the spice burger fast became a Dublin chipper classic that is now available in many parts of the east of Ireland and has become a frequent addition to lunchtime tables and dinner plates for the last few generations. We have such vivid, fond memories of this deep-fried delicacy that's heavily herbed and spiced with its meat-meets-breadcrumb bouncy texture and hockey puck heft. The food processor is your friend here – in fact, it's essential to achieve the correct texture.

sunflower or vegetable oil, for deep-frying

350g beef steak mince

1 small white onion, peeled and roughly chopped

60g fresh breadcrumbs

1½ tbsp herbes de Provence or dried mixed herbs

2 tsp fine sea salt

1½ tsp cayenne pepper

1½ tsp ground white pepper

drizzle of olive oil

30g plain flour

1 egg, beaten

50g dried breadcrumbs

TO SERVE:

flaky sea salt

malt vinegar

Heat the oil in your deep-fryer to 170°C.

Place the beef mince and onion in a food processor and continuously pulse until choppily combined. Add the fresh breadcrumbs, herbes de Provence or dried mixed herbs, salt, cayenne and white pepper and continue to pulse until everything is evenly incorporated. With the motor running, drizzle in a little olive oil just until the mixture forms into a ball, then stop.

Remove from the food processor and form into a flat round, akin to making a traditional Irish soda bread, and eyeball it into four equal quadrants (roughly 120g each). Shape into neat hockey puck shapes about 4cm thick that fit cosily in the palm of your hand.

Prepare your pané station with three separate wide, shallow dishes: one for the flour (stir through a little seasoning), another for the beaten egg and the third for the dried breadcrumbs. Cover each burger with flour on all sides, shaking off any excess, then submerge into the beaten egg before covering entirely in an even layer of dried breadcrumbs.

Working in batches if necessary, fry the burgers in the hot oil for 5 minutes, flipping halfway through, especially if they peek over the oil line. Place on a wire rack set over a baking tray lined with kitchen paper to absorb any excess oil. Adorn with a final seasoning of flaky sea salt and chip shop (malt) vinegar.

SPICE BURGERS ≠ SPICE BAGS

Name aside, this bears no sibling synonymity
with the spice bag on page 56, which is another
takeaway staple but very different in the form of
spiced chicken and chips. This is simply served and
eaten as is, rather than in a bun like other burgers.

TURKEY SCHNITZEL

SERVES 2

Schnitzel is the German word for its French counterpart, escalope – a pounded piece of meat, coated and then fried. The Austrians lay a big claim to schnitzel, and actually Wiener Schnitzel is the proper, traditional method, which always uses veal. We're putting a twist on the schnitzel technique and changing the protein to turkey, which we think works wonderfully here. This is so easy that we regularly have it as an effortless midweek dinner.

Staying in Central Europe for a moment, we spent some time in Frankfurt a couple of years back and had Frankfurter schnitzel with boiled potatoes and Grie Soß, a PGI-designated green sauce using seven different herbs local to Frankfurt: parsley, cress, borage, chervil, chive, burnet (or lemon balm) and sorrel. These are pounded to a paste and made into a mayonnaise or stirred through sour cream to make a sprightly sidekick sauce that goes so well with schnitzel. Alternatively, serve this with a sharply dressed side salad.

We suggest you use a large frying pan rather than a deep-fryer here, as the larger-than-life size of the flattened fillet just doesn't work in a conventional home fryer.

2 x 120g pieces of turkey breast fillet

200ml sunflower oil

50g plain flour

1 large egg + a splash of milk to thin

150g fine dried breadcrumbs

fine sea salt and ground white pepper

The sauce is best made at least an hour in advance, if not a full day, to give the herbs a chance to soften and infuse their flavour. The hand chopping can be tedious, but don't be tempted to use a food processor as it will break down and bruise the delicate leaves – a sharp knife and patience are your best tools. Add all the herbs and spring onion tops to the crème fraîche or sour cream and stir through the lemon juice and seasoning. Taste and adjust the seasoning if need be, then thin it a little to your desired consistency with the buttermilk, milk or water. Cover and keep in the fridge until ready to serve.

Using a rolling pin or meat pounder, bash each piece of turkey between two sheets of cling film until it's about 1.5cm thick.

Heat the oil in a heavy-based, wide frying pan over a medium heat as you prepare your pané station with three separate wide, shallow dishes: a dish for the flour, a dish for the egg and milk whisked together and a dish for the breadcrumbs.

FOR THE GREEN SAUCE:

a small handful each of cress (or young watercress), parsley, sorrel, chives, borage, lemon balm and chervil, all very finely chopped by hand

2 spring onions, green tops only, very thinly sliced

200ml crème fraîche or sour cream

juice of ¼ lemon

fine sea salt and ground white pepper

a little buttermilk, milk or water, to thin

TO SERVE:

flaky sea salt

lemon wedges

fresh salad leaves with a sharp dressing

Season the pounded turkey breasts generously on both sides before coating in the flour, shaking off any excess. Turn to coat in the egg wash and finally coat fully in the breadcrumbs. If you'd like a double coating, return the breadcrumb-adorned schnitzel to the egg and once again into the breadcrumbs (you may need extra eggs and breadcrumbs for this).

Place gently into the hot oil (always lowered in angled away from yourself) and jiggle the pan a little to ensure it doesn't stick to the bottom. Cook for 2–3 minutes, then using sturdy tongs, carefully turn over and cook on the second side for 2–3 minutes more.

Place on a wire rack set over a baking tray lined with kitchen paper to absorb any excess oil and sprinkle over some flaky sea salt. Serve while still warm with the green sauce, a lemon wedge for squeezing over and a sharply dressed salad on the side.

BUTTERMILK FRIED CHICKEN BURGERS

MAKES 4

Can you taste quality? We think so. In fact, we've made a point of it in our food writing since we began almost a decade ago now: whatever your budget, buy the best quality you can because – trust us – it comes through in the end product. Same goes for using the freshest ingredients you can find and for buying in season. Chicken is no exception – free-range is a real sticking point for us. You can absolutely tell the difference between battery and free-range, especially in recipes where the chicken meat is the star and the main draw. Mini TED Talk over.

This recipe takes some time and has a few steps, but by the end of it all, you will have the crispest, most flavoursome fried chicken you can imagine. We recommend using breasts for a burger, but skinless, boneless thighs work just as well and will cook a tiny bit quicker.

250ml buttermilk

1 tsp fine sea salt

½ tsp freshly ground black pepper

¼ tsp MSG (optional)

4 free-range chicken breasts, flattened

sunflower oil, for deep-frying

1 large egg

25ml milk

70g plain flour

70g rice flour

70g potato starch

1 tbsp dried mixed herbs (we use herbes de Provence)

1 tsp cracked black pepper

½ tbsp sweet smoked paprika

¼ tsp cayenne pepper

Pour your buttermilk into a bowl or deep dish and whisk in the salt, black pepper and MSG (if using). Submerge your chicken into it, cover with cling film and leave in the fridge for at least 3 hours, but you can leave it overnight. This will tenderise the meat beautifully and add the initial wet 'coating'.

After the brining time, take your chicken out of the fridge and allow to come to room temperature in the dish for about half an hour.

Heat the oil in your deep-fryer to around 150°C, which is on the lower scale but this is a two-stage fry. While vegetable oil works absolutely fine, we find that sunflower oil is better for this particular recipe.

Set up your pané station. In one wide, shallow bowl, whisk the egg and milk together. In another bowl, combine the flours and potato starch with the mixed dried herbs, black pepper, sweet smoked paprika and cayenne pepper. Take about one-third of the seasoned flour and put it in a third bowl. (So to recap: one bowl for the egg and milk, one bowl with two-thirds of the seasoned flour and one bowl with one-third of the seasoned flour.)

TO SERVE:

burger buns or wraps

mayonnaise

shredded lettuce

sliced tomatoes

thinly sliced red onion rings

hot sauce

sliced cheese

Working with one fillet at a time, remove the chicken from the buttermilk mixture, giving it a little shake to remove the excess, then coat in the bowl that has one-third of the seasoned flour. Next, coat it in the egg mixture, then dredge it in the bowl that has two-thirds of the flour, ensuring full coverage in every crack and crevice.

With the fryer basket already lowered, gently introduce the chicken into the fryer. Cook each piece for 6–7 minutes, depending on the size. You can cook in batches of two at once if your fryer is big enough, otherwise cook individually. Shake off the excess oil, then place on a wire rack set over a baking tray lined with kitchen paper.

When all the chicken has had its first dip in the oil, crank the temperature up to 190°C for the second fry. When the oil has come up to temperature, lower the chicken into the oil once more and fry for 90 seconds or so, until golden and crisp.

Serve between burger buns with mayo, shredded lettuce, tomato, red onion, hot sauce and cheese, or slice into strips and enjoy in a similarly stuffed wrap.

HOW TO REHEAT

These burgers actually reheat quite well. Cover the cooked chicken in an airtight container and store it in the fridge for up to a day or two, then reheat on a wire rack set over a baking tray in a 200°C oven or at 180°C in an air fryer for 10–12 minutes, until completely heated through.

BUTTERMILK FRIED CHICKEN VARIATIONS

1 PICKLE-BRINED

If you love the sweet, salty hit that brine gives in more places than just a dirty martini, here's one for you: substitute some of the buttermilk for pickle brine from your favourite jar of pickles or gherkins – try using 150ml buttermilk and 100ml brine.

2 TEA-BRINED

Tea brines are also used to bring more flavour to the chicken and are worth exploring further if you wish. A bit more time intensive, often taking about 24 hours to be ready to fry, but the flavour is worth it.

3 SPICED

Don't be afraid to increase the piquancy of your dried spices in the seasoned flour: think hot smoked paprika, cayenne pepper, gochugaru or red chilli flakes. Or try curry powder or garam masala – make of this what you want!

4 HOT SAUCE

For something hot, you can add 2 tablespoons of hot sauce to your egg and milk mixture when coating your chicken for a fiery layer of spice.

5 NASHVILLE FRIED CHICKEN

A really popular variation of a spicy fried chicken right now is Nashville fried chicken. After the final fry, the chicken is glazed in a blend of about 1½ tablespoons cayenne pepper, ½ tablespoon brown sugar, 1 teaspoon garlic powder, ½ teaspoon sweet smoked paprika and ½ teaspoon chilli powder, all whisked together with about two ladlefuls of the hot fat from the fryer.

6 BAHARAT

We are fond of using a spice blend commonly used around the Middle East called baharat (allspice, cinnamon, cardamom, cumin, coriander, peppercorns and more), available in specialist food stores, including Mezze in Tramore, County Waterford, and online. In place of the herbs and spices in our fried chicken recipe, we use 1½ tablespoons of this blend in the flour and starch mix, plus about 1 teaspoon of salt. Serve this alongside a fermented hot sauce, something cooling like tzatziki and a warm flatbread.

7 CHEESY

Whatever way you fry your chicken, don't be afraid to customise it as you please. Experiment with different sauces, ketchups or mayos as you build up your flavours, depending on how you want to serve the chicken. Play around with cheeses too. One of our favourite things to make is a cheat's nacho sauce by melting a couple of squares of sliced processed cheese over a low heat in a saucepan with a tablespoon or two of water, magically becoming a bright orange sauce. We also add 1 teaspoon of mustard and ¼ teaspoon of turmeric, then pour it all over the hot fried chicken.

KOREAN FRIED CHICKEN

SERVES A GREEDY 2

We make no apologies for the fact that we're led almost exclusively by our tastebuds when we travel, pinpointing bucket list bites and food and drink experiences we *need* to discover, squeezed into every second of exploring. A recent two-week trip to South Korea was happily spent between Seoul and Busan chowing down on Korean fried chicken several times daily to find the best. Sofie and Garret of Chimac in Dublin gave us their own blueprint for the best-found fried chicken in Seoul (and if you're in Dublin, we really recommend trying their versions!).

What makes KFC different? A couple of things: crucially, a blend of flours and starches and it's double fried, the combination of which results in a shatteringly crisp coating that is then smothered in a fiery, punchy, sticky, crimson-coloured sauce that still retains its crisp as you eat. Talk about finger-lickin' good! This is next level – napkins at the ready.

6–8 boneless, skinless chicken thighs

300ml buttermilk

2 tsp gochugaru or paprika

sunflower or vegetable oil, for deep-frying

FOR THE COATING:

60g plain flour

60g rice flour

60g potato starch or cornflour

1 tsp baking powder

sea salt and freshly ground black pepper

Cut each chicken thigh into two or three pieces to make bite-sized chunks and season with salt. Whisk the buttermilk and gochugaru or paprika together in a large bowl or baking dish. Submerge all the chicken in the buttermilk, cover with cling film and marinate in the fridge for a good 4–6 hours (leaving it overnight is fine too).

When it's time to cook, remove the buttermilk-brined chicken from the fridge about 30 minutes before frying. Heat the oil in your deep-fryer to 150°C.

Combine all the coating ingredients in one bowl. (If you've run out of baking powder, use 60g self-raising flour instead of the plain flour.)

Working quickly and without shaking off too much of the buttermilk, dredge the chicken pieces in the flour mix, ensuring a generous and even coating. Working in batches, add each piece directly into the fryer and cook for about 5 minutes, until cooked through and light golden. Remove from the fryer and set aside on a wire rack set over a baking tray lined with kitchen paper while you cook the rest of the chicken.

FOR THE SAUCE:

4 tbsp rice wine vinegar or Shaoxing rice wine

2 tbsp gochujang

2 tbsp sriracha

2 tbsp tomato ketchup

2 tbsp caster sugar

1 tbsp sesame oil

1 tbsp aekjeot or nam pla fish sauce

1 tbsp gochugaru

1 tbsp honey

1 tbsp butter

TO GARNISH:

sesame seeds

spring onions, sliced into thin lengths or on an angle

thinly sliced or chopped fresh red or green chilli

When all the pieces have had their first fry and have been drained, crank up the temperature of the oil to 190°C.

Meanwhile, put all the sauce ingredients in a saucepan set over a medium heat and bring to the boil, then drop down to the lowest heat setting and give it a stir every so often just to keep it warm and pourable.

Fry all the chicken for a second time for 90 seconds to 2 minutes, until it looks incredibly crisp and has darkened in colour. Depending on the size of your fryer basket, you may need to do this in two batches.

Place the chicken into a large heatproof bowl and pour over all the sauce, tossing to coat each piece. The chicken will soak up the sauce but still retain its crispness.

Plate up with a generous sprinkle of sesame seeds, sliced spring onions and fresh chilli on top. Alternatively, serve in a steamed bao or as a burger. Kimchi or some sharp pickles are the ideal supporting side act or you can go all out on the whole banchan experience of a table laden with small side dishes.

WHAT IS GOCHUJANG?

Gochugaru is piquant Korean chilli pepper flakes, aekjeot is a Korean fish sauce and gochujang is an iconic Korean chilli paste. The aekjeot and gochugaru have natural alternatives but there's really no substitute for the intensely sticky, fiery gochujang paste, which is integral to recipe. However, you should be able to find all these ingredients at your nearest Asian market.

SPEEDY CHICKEN NUGGS

MAKES 8

For when you crave chicken nuggets and nothing else will do – the quickest we've completed this is 20 minutes. The flavour is pure chicken, the coating is light and the texture has that crucial bounce we all associate with nuggs. These are deliciously dunkable, so dip these bad boys into a homemade sauce – see pages 54–55 for a handful of really simple support act sauce recipes.

sunflower or vegetable oil, for deep-frying

1 free-range chicken breast fillet (roughly 140–150g), cut into cubes (turkey breast also works well)

1½ tbsp full-fat cream cheese

½ tsp fine sea salt

½ tsp freshly ground black pepper

TO COAT:

1 large egg

1 tbsp hot sauce (optional)

60g plain flour, divided between two bowls (30g + 30g)

½ tsp sweet smoked paprika

½ tsp freshly ground black pepper

TO SERVE:

flaky sea salt

your favourite dip (see pages 54–55)

Heat the oil in your deep-fryer to 170°C.

Put the chicken, cream cheese and salt and pepper in a food processor and blend to a paste.

Prepare your pané station with three separate wide, shallow bowls. Whisk the egg in one bowl. (If you want to bring some heat to the party, add 1 tablespoon of your favourite hot sauce to the whisked egg and to give the nuggets an extra piquant punch!)

Divide the flour evenly between two other wide, shallow bowls. Add the paprika and black pepper to one of the bowls and keep the other bowl of flour plain. Line up your three bowls: the plain flour, your egg mixture and your seasoned flour.

Keep a little dish of water nearby, as slicking your hands with water before shaping makes this a lot less messy. Form the mixture into approximately eight equal-sized oval rounds, about one-third the size of your palm and the thickness of your little finger. Dredge through the plain flour, then the egg mixture and finally coat in the seasoned flour, leaving them all on a clean plate or tray in preparation for frying.

Fry in batches of four in the hot oil for 4–5 minutes, until golden and crisp. Raise the basket from the oil and shake off the excess oil.

Serve while still warm with a little flaky sea salt sprinkled on top and your favourite dip to accompany.

DELICIOUSLY DUNKABLE

STICKY BBQ SAUCE

75g dark brown sugar

½ tbsp tomato purée

125ml water

2–4 dashes Worcestershire sauce

4 tbsp apple cider vinegar or red wine vinegar

2 tbsp soy sauce

1½ tsp sweet smoked paprika

¼ tsp cayenne pepper

¼ tsp fine sea salt

$1/8$ tsp freshly ground black pepper

2 tsp cornflour, whisked with a little milk to loosen to a pouring consistency

Bring all the ingredients except the cornflour to the boil in a saucepan, then lower the heat to medium-low. Allow to reduce and thicken over the course of 10–15 minutes, stirring every so often. When the liquid has almost entirely evaporated, add the cornflour mixture. Allow the sauce to get sticky and thick to the point of coating a spoon, noting that this will thicken further when cooled. Store in a sterilised jar or airtight container for up to one week in the fridge if not using immediately.

RANCH

4 tbsp mayonnaise

2 tbsp buttermilk

1 tsp finely chopped fresh chives

1 tsp mixed dried herbs

¼ tsp fine sea salt

¼ tsp freshly ground black pepper

Whisk together all the ingredients and taste for seasoning. Allow to rest, covered, in the fridge for around 1 hour before you use it to allow the flavour to build and to thicken up a little. Creamy, herby and sharp, ranch also works wonderfully as a thin dressing for salads or sandwiches. If you find the mixture too thin, you could stir through some créme fraîche to thicken.

SWEET CURRY SAUCE

75ml water

20ml orange juice

4 tbsp apricot jam

2 tbsp white wine vinegar

½ tsp tomato purée

30g caster sugar

1 tbsp mild curry powder

1 tsp fine sea salt

1½ tsp cornflour, whisked with a little milk to loosen to a pouring consistency

Whisk the water, orange juice, apricot jam, vinegar and tomato purée together in a saucepan over a medium-high heat. Bring to the boil, then reduce to a simmer and add the sugar, curry powder and salt. Cook for 10–15 minutes, stirring regularly, allowing it to bubble down and thicken. Towards the end, add the cornflour mixture and keep reducing until you get a sauce the consistency of thick ketchup, noting that this will thicken slightly further when cooled. Store in a sterilised jar or airtight container for up to one week in the fridge if not using immediately.

HONEY MUSTARD

juice of ½ lemon

3 tbsp mayonnaise

3 tbsp Dijon mustard

1 tbsp runny honey

¼ tsp ground white pepper

a pinch of salt

a couple sprigs of fresh thyme, leaves removed

Whisk together all the ingredients and taste for seasoning. Allow to rest, covered, in the fridge for around 1 hour before you use it to allow the flavour to build and to thicken up a little.

SWEET CHILLI SAUCE

150g caster sugar

75ml apple cider or white wine vinegar

1 fresh red chilli, deseeded and very finely diced

1 garlic clove, grated

1 piece of fresh ginger a similar size as the garlic clove, peeled and grated

a pinch of salt

2 tbsp water + 1 tsp cornflour, mixed

Bring the sugar, vinegar, chilli, garlic, ginger and salt to the boil in a small saucepan over a medium heat, then reduce the heat to medium-low and stir through the cornflour mixture. Allow to reduce and thicken to a jam-like consistency, then remove from the heat and allow to cool before serving.

SPICE BAG

SERVES 4

Crisp chicken pieces tumbled with chips, wok-fried vegetables, chilli and garlic, all dusted in a signature spice seasoning and served in a brown paper bag. Though its origins point to the south-western suburbs of Dublin City, pretty much every Asian takeaway in the country has their own interpretation of the spice bag. It's so popular that it's become the No. 1 takeaway dish in recent years. Although it's arguably just a combination of the most commonly ordered 'Western' elements packaged together and called something new, this is truly tastebud tantalising – the ultimate combination of hot, sweet and salty.

8 boneless, skinless chicken thighs (or 3–4 chicken breasts), sliced into long, thin strips

175ml buttermilk (or regular milk + 2 tsp freshly squeezed lemon juice)

75g plain flour

sunflower or vegetable oil, for deep-frying

4 large chipping potatoes, peeled (Kerr's Pinks, Maris Pipers and Roosters all work well)

2 medium-sized white onions, sliced into 1cm-thick half-moons

3–4 fresh red chillies, sliced (deseeding is optional)

8 garlic cloves, finely chopped

Soak the chicken in the buttermilk in a bowl while you get on with everything else. This will tenderise and also coat the chicken for the next stage.

Mix together all the ingredients for the spice bag blend.

Put the flour in a wide-lipped bowl or plate and stir in 1 or 2 tablespoons of the spice bag blend. Set aside.

To make the chips, heat the oil in your deep-fryer to 160°C and follow the recipe for the perfect chips on page 29 up till the end of the first fry.

When you're ready to fry the chicken, remove each piece from the buttermilk and lightly shake off any excess, then dunk it into the seasoned flour and gently lower into the hot oil (still at 160°C). You may need to do this in two or three batches. Depending on size, the chicken will take around 5 minutes per batch – it's done when the pieces are golden brown and crisp. Drain using the basket, then remove to a wire rack set over a baking tray lined with kitchen paper.

Crank the oil up to 190°C for the final flash fry of the chips while you stir-fry the vegetables.

FOR THE SPICE BAG BLEND:

1 tbsp five-spice powder

2 tsp granulated sugar

2 tsp fine sea salt

1 tsp chilli powder

1 tsp Szechuan peppercorns, ground (optional if, like us, you love the mouth-numbing sensation)

½ tsp garlic powder

⅛ tsp ground cardamom

⅛ tsp ground cinnamon

⅛ tsp ground ginger

½ tsp ground white pepper

TO SERVE:

ready-made Chinese curry sauce

Heat ½ tablespoon of oil in a wok or large frying pan over a high heat. Add the onions, then the chillies and garlic, and quickly fry, keeping them moving regularly. This should take only 1 minute or less, as you're just softening them rather than cooking out – a little crunch and bite are essential. Remove from the heat in advance of plating up.

Fry the chips for a further 60–90 seconds at the higher temperature to get your desired golden shade, then drain well and immediately add to a large metal mixing bowl with the chicken and the vegetables. Sprinkle over 1– 2 tablespoons of the spice bag blend, then shake it all together – this will help to cool things down and will also keep the chips crisp as you keep everything moving and add air.

Serve hot, with or without curry sauce to accompany. We definitely fall into the 'with' category, but we know some perfectly entitled purists prefer it 'dry' style.

APPLE HAND PIES

MAKES 6

Hand-held desserts, what a concept! This crunchy, crisp, hand-held pie sings with its sweet spiced filling and is super easy to put together. You can play around with your choice of fruit (rhubarb, plum, cherries), but good old green apple is the ultimate classic.

3 medium green apples, peeled, cored and cut into small cubes

50g light brown sugar

juice of ½ lemon

1 tbsp cornflour

1 tbsp ground cinnamon

½ tsp ground nutmeg or mace

¼ tsp ground cardamom

fresh sunflower or vegetable oil, for deep-frying

icing sugar, for dusting

1 sheet of pre-rolled puff pastry (all-butter if possible)

FOR THE CINNAMON SUGAR TOPPING:

80g granulated sugar

1 heaped tsp ground cinnamon

Add the cubed apples, brown sugar, lemon juice, cornflour and spices to a saucepan with a drop of water and cook down on a medium-low heat for 20 minutes, stirring every so often to avoid it sticking or burning. You don't want it to turn to mush – you still want a little bit of texture and structure from the apples. Set aside to cool.

Heat the oil in your deep-fryer or a high-sided pan to 170°C. As this is a sweet recipe, we recommend using fresh oil rather than using a fryer full of oil that has been anointed with all manner of spicy chicken, onion rings and frites.

Sift a bit of icing sugar over a clean work surface and roll out the sheet of puff pastry to an even thickness (about 3mm), then cut into six rectangles about 10cm x 15cm.

In each rectangle, dollop 3 teaspoons of the filling along the long side, off centre, as you're going to seal it by folding over the other half. Take a small pastry brush and dab a little water around the edges of the open pastry. Fold the empty side over the filling, then crimp with the tines of a fork to seal.

Working with a maximum of two pies at a time (depending on the size of your fryer), carefully place the pies in the hot oil and cook for 8 minutes.

Meanwhile, to make the topping, mix the sugar and cinnamon together in a wide, shallow dish or pasta bowl.

Remove the pies from the fryer and shake the basket
to allow the excess oil to drain for a few seconds, then
dredge the pie(s) in the cinnamon sugar while still hot.
Set on a wire rack and enjoy after a couple of minutes
– resist the temptation to dive right in, as the molten
middle will make itself known!

DEEP-FRIED ICE CREAM

MAKES AROUND 6

You read it right: deep-fried ice cream. It's like a baked Alaska, except more blow-out and brilliant. Hot, cold, crisp, soft, melting, crunchy, the flavours of biscuit and cereal just echoing in the background. This is a time-consuming one but also quite hands-off. It just takes a couple of stages and an unbelievably miniscule amount of time actually immersed in hot fat, but the result ... mother of God, this is dessert with decadence and the volume turned up to piercing levels.

Remember, this is achievable but counterintuitive as you are immersing something frozen and solid into blazing hot oil, so take our advice: make sure the coating is thick and covers every bit of the ice cream within. And speaking of the coating, play around with your choice of cereal. We adore the peanut-flecked crunchy flaked variety, but we also love chocolate pops! Have fun with your melting middle ice cream variety too.

1 tub or block of your choice of ice cream

5–8 digestive biscuits

50–70g of your favourite cereal (see the intro)

1 large egg

1 tbsp milk

fresh sunflower or vegetable oil, for deep-frying

TO SERVE:

honey or maple syrup

icing sugar

fresh mint

Several hours before you want to make this, take your ice cream out of the freezer and either scoop it out using an ice cream scoop or cut it into blocks if taking it from a rectangular box – uniformity is important, whatever you do. Place the portions on a tray or board and refreeze for at least 1 hour.

Crush the biscuits in a ziplock bag with a rolling pin until they are basically dust (you can of course use a food processor if you have one). Transfer to a mixing bowl.

Do the same thing to the cereal, then place it in a separate mixing bowl and set this bowl aside for later.

Remove the ice cream from the freezer. Using a palette knife and working with one portion at a time, remove the ice cream from the frozen plate and place into the biscuit dust. Using two forks or dessertspoons (to avoid excess touching, as the ice cream may be very fragile and soft), roll the ice cream to cover it in the dust, making sure there are no gaps, then place back into the freezer for 1 hour.

Whisk the egg and milk together in a dish or bowl.

Working quickly, remove the ice cream freezer. One by one, place once again into the crushed biscuits, then into the egg wash, then dredge in the cereal. A double, if not triple, coating is essential, so put each portion back into the egg, then back into the cereal and freeze for a further 3 hours or overnight. If leaving it for any longer, loosely cover with cling film.

When it comes to frying time, heat the fresh oil in your deep-fryer to 190°C.

When you're ready, remove the ice cream from the freezer and place directly into the oil for 10–15 seconds. Yes, seconds.

Remove, drain very quickly and serve, drizzling some honey or maple syrup, a dusting of icing sugar and a bit of fresh mint on top for good measure. Apply to face.

DOUGHNUTS

MAKES 12–15

Originally called oily cakes and most likely brought to the States by Dutch settlers in the early 19th century, you might wonder whether they should now be spelled doughnut or donut. Well, doughnut is the original word, whereas the shortened, simplified donut spelling has been knocking around since the 20th century. Both are used interchangeably today.

Doughnuts have a diverse culinary lineage, with many iterations found around the world. In Germany and Austria, they're called Berliner or Krapfen. Likewise in parts of northern Italy, whereas in Tuscany they're known as bombolini. In Portugal, a popular treat at pastelaria (and commonly, but somewhat unusually, at the beach) is bola de Berlim, which are doughnuts filled with a thick yellow sweet egg curd called creme de pasteleiro. The oven-baked pampushky of Ukraine are believed to have been an adaptation of Krapfen, while in the Balkan countries krofne or krofi are similar, but usually come filled with an apricot jam.

1 x 7g sachet of fast-action dried yeast

50g caster sugar

125ml warm water

400g strong white flour, plus extra for dusting

1 tsp fine sea salt

3 large eggs

80g butter, cubed and very soft

fresh sunflower or vegetable oil, for deep-frying

100g granulated sugar

1 tsp ground cardamom

1 tsp ground cinnamon

Bloom the yeast with the sugar in a bowl or jug of the warm water, stirring to combine. Allow to bubble up for 10 minutes while you put the flour and salt into the bowl of your stand mixer fitted with a dough hook.

Add the yeasted water mixture into the flour along with the eggs and gradually incorporate, beginning on a low speed and incrementally going up to medium (so you don't end up wearing the flour!) and allowing the dough hook to work the mixture on medium for 15 minutes. You'll notice the dough coming away from the sides of the bowl and bearing long, sticky but fairly stable gluten strands. Turn off the mixer and allow the dough to rest for 5 minutes, covered.

Begin the mixer again on medium speed and add your softened butter cube by cube until it's all entirely incorporated and a smooth, sticky dough forms. Cover the bowl and allow the dough to prove until it has doubled in size. As this is an enriched dough, this may take several hours.

Knock the dough back and allow to rest for 5 minutes. Using lightly floured hands, tip the dough out of the bowl and

onto a lightly floured work surface. Portion into 50–60g pieces and roll into balls – you should get anywhere between 12 and 15 doughnuts. Without adding too much flour (flouring your hands should be enough), roll out each ball until it's taut and round, then place each finished doughnut onto a lightly floured, lipped baking tray to prove for a second time. You may need two to four trays, as you want these to be spaced out enough so that they don't touch and merge into one as they prove. Cover in lightly greased cling film (which ensures that they won't stick as they grow!) and allow to prove for a further few hours until doubled in size. Alternatively, at this point you could put these into the fridge on the trays and slowly prove overnight or for 8–10 hours.

Heat the fresh oil in your deep-fryer to 170°C.

Stir together the sugar and spices in a lipped tray or bowl for post-frying doughnut dips and get familiar with your dough scraper – drawn

through a bit of extra flour, it will help you get the leverage you need to carefully transfer the delicate puffed doughnuts to the hot oil without losing all that precious air inside.

Working in small batches, place directly into the hot oil (rather than in the basket and then lowered) and fry for roughly 2 minutes per side, turning once to ensure an even, light golden colour on the top and bottom, with a distinct white line running around the middle.

Drain using the basket or a frying spider, shaking off any excess oil, then roll in the spiced sugar while still warm. Put the doughnuts on a clean dish or baking tray, covered with a clean tea towel to stop them from hardening and drying out, while you make the rest.

If not eating these on the same day, allow them to cool completely, store in an airtight container and consume within three days.

TRY THESE

DOUGHNUT FILLINGS

If you want to fill the doughnuts, wait until they are cold and make sure you fill them with a cooled mixture – whether you use a thickened custard, curd, whipped cream or seedless jam is up to you. Use a chopstick to make a hole on one side along the 'line' through to the middle of the doughnut and wiggle it a bit to create more space inside for filling. Use a piping bag with a nozzle attachment to fill your doughnut, ensuring the filling isn't runny – rather, it should be thick and stable. Fill to the brim and it's always nice to add a generous dot on top of the opening, a hint to the prospective eater of the flavour to be found within! Each of these fillings can be made and kept refrigerated for up to two days before you need to use it.

LEMON & LIME CURD

125g caster sugar

3 egg yolks

1 whole egg

2 tbsp cornflour

juice of 3 lemons

juice of 3 limes

75g butter, diced into roughly 5g cubes, softened

Whisk the sugar, egg yolks, the whole egg and the cornflour together. Continue whisking as you introduce the citrus juice, then transfer to a saucepan on a very low heat and stir often until it begins to thicken.

Add the butter cube by cube, adding each one only after the last has been incorporated. Once all the butter has been added, increase the heat a small bit and whisk vigorously as the mixture begins to thicken to the consistency of lightly whipped double cream.

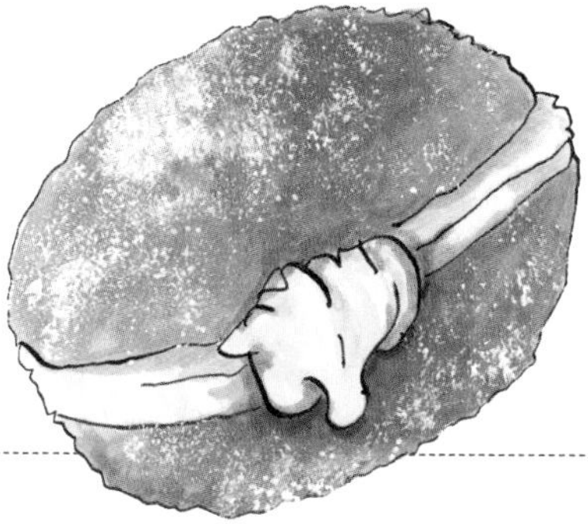

COFFEE CRÈME PÂTISSIÈRE

125g caster sugar

25g plain flour

25g cornflour

4 large or 6 medium egg yolks

50ml cooled espresso

300ml milk

Combine the sugar, flour, cornflour and egg yolks in a bowl, stirring to a thick eggy mixture, then add the cooled espresso.

Heat the milk in a saucepan on a medium heat until it just comes to the boil, then remove from the heat, add one-third of the warm milk into the egg mixture and whisk vigorously to incorporate. Pour this back into the saucepan and return to a medium heat. Keep stirring or whisking as it comes back up to temperature and begins to thicken. As it thickens you can gradually increase the heat, but have patience with this and don't succumb to heating it too high too early, as it could boil and split. Ensure you're scraping the bottom in case any of the mixture is catching, as this is a sign it's too hot. After a couple of minutes you will have a very thick custard, which will thicken slightly further as it cools. Keep in a jug or bowl with a layer of cling film directly touching the surface to stop a skin forming until needed.

INDEX

Nine Bean Rows Books

23 Mountjoy Square

Dublin 1, Ireland

@9beanrowsbooks

ninebeanrowsbooks.com

NINE
BEAN
ROWS

Blasta Books is an imprint of Nine Bean Rows Books Ltd.

@blastabooks blastabooks.com

First published 2022

ISBN: 978-1-9993799-1-9

Editor: Kristin Jensen

Series artist: Nicky Hooper
nickyhooper.com

Designer: Jane Matthews
janematthewsdesign.com

Proofreader: Jocelyn Doyle

Printed by L&C Printing Group, Poland